100

THINGS TO DO IN

RENO

BEFORE YOU

DIE

100
THINGS TO DO IN
RENO
BEFORE YOU
DIE

• •

MIKALEE BYERMAN

REEDY PRESS

Reedy Press
PO Box 5131
St. Louis, MO 63139, USA
www.reedypress.com

Library of Congress Control Number: 2016955745

ISBN: 9781681060675

Design by Jill Halpin

Special thanks to the Reno-Sparks Convention and Visitors Authority and The Terry Lee Wells Nevada Discovery Museum for editorial photos, and to Jeff Dow Photography for the author photo

Printed in the United States of America
17 18 19 20 21   5 4 3 2

DEDICATION

To Reno.

For providing a spectacularly loving community and welcoming home for the most important people in my world: my beautiful children, my parents, my family, and all of my friends.

We are blessed to know you.

CONTENTS

Music and Entertainment

• •

Sports, Recreation, and Outdoor Adventure

• •

Culture and History

• •

Shopping and Fashion

● ●

PREFACE

Full disclosure: This has been like the Sophie's Choice of book projects. I'm not even kidding. I have spent the last six months making notes in my iPhone every time I pass a place worthy of mention, such that when it came time to start writing, I had about 14,324 experiences to share. Give or take.

Enter Sophie's Choice. Which ones should I keep? Which ones do I dismiss? How will that make the others feel? Poor, poor dejected choices.

But alas: The book called for 100 Things, and so I was compelled to deliver. (There may be some cheating ahead, because in some cases, I grouped by category. Smart, right?)

So, anyhow: I love this book. And yet I hate this book. Because for every entry, there are places I had to forgo. But this love-hate relationship has reminded me often that this was never intended to be the be-all, end-all comprehensive guide to what makes Reno tick. That would take volumes. This is just 100 experiences as curated by me, a middle-aged single mom, a writer, a lover of Reno, a two-time graduate of the University of Nevada, Reno, a woman who distrusts tapioca pudding because of the nubs. Everything in that previous sentence ultimately serves to impact the filter through which I chose these experiences.

• •

Spoiler alert: there are no places listed in this book that shine a spotlight on tapioca pudding. My apologies if that's your thing and now you're sad.

I wrote this book as a reflection of my passion for this community—a community that has wrapped my family in a comfortable blanket of nourishment for years. I am so grateful to live here, and I've never been more excited by the possibilities to come. So please, if I missed experiences in this book, ones you wished I had mentioned: I wish I could have mentioned them, too. And perhaps there will be updates, books of 100 more things, online interactive conversations, apps, or future opportunities. Because as Reno continues to evolve, demand will grow for more chances to explore all it has to offer.

In the meantime: join me at "100 Things to Do in Reno Before You Die" on Facebook. Tell me about your experiences with this book, using the hashtag #100Reno. I'm so excited to hear your feedback and to prepare for the next chapter—literally and figuratively.

And thank you from the bottom of my heart for reading this book. I hope you enjoy it even half as much as I enjoyed writing it.

Even if it practically broke my Reno-loving heart every time I was confronted with another example of Mikalee's Choice.

ACKNOWLEDGMENTS

I feel so blessed to be a member of my crazy village. I am surrounded by the most encouraging and loving family and friends, and for that, I wish to thank you all from the bottom of my heart. I need to say it again: I feel so blessed.

Thank you first and foremost to my children. Dylan, you were finishing up your senior year of high school as I wrote most of this book, and I know there were times when you needed me to order another set of ACT scores or proof another scholarship app. And I sincerely hope you never felt pushed aside, because I've spent this entire year just wanting to pull you ever closer before you leave the nest! Please know that I could not possibly be any prouder of you and how you've navigated this crazy year. You're the pioneer of the family, my firstborn, and my only son. I love you more than you'll ever know.

To Jilleann, you were just starting high school as I wrote most of this book, and yet I feel like you've always been right by my side this entire time. Actually, you've pretty much *literally* been right there, as we've spent countless miles together on the road, talking about days and experiences and volleyball and friends and basketball and vocab lists. Our car conversations are my favorite. Your grace, charm, and beautiful spirit always help shine a light, even when things seem overwhelming. Please know I respect, love, and admire you more than you'll ever know. I only wish I will someday be as fierce as you.

To The Bryerlee: Just wow. You had no idea I was even writing this book, you in your perfectly appropriate self-centered toddlerhood, and yet—you provided so much unexpected love and compassion, I can't even begin to understand. You're a force of nature, and all of our lives are so much better off because you're here. Thank you for cooking me endless dinners in your play kitchen while I wrote. Thank you for entertaining yourself—and frequently, me—while I wrote. You take my breath away, every single day.

To my parents, Jim and Sharon: I can't even imagine what I've done in life to deserve your unconditional love and support. Even in the most difficult of times, I've always known you were there by my side, my loudest cheerleaders, reminding me to sleep, making sure I was consuming more than Diet Coke each day. I'm so grateful. And of course, I'm especially grateful for the help with the aforementioned children—especially that force of nature. We all love you so much.

To my brother David and his beautiful family—Caroline, Amanda, and Will—you may be far away, but you're always in my heart. Nevada misses you! To my BFF Karena, thank you for always asking how my book was going and for being such a constant, engaging presence in my life. And I'm still sorry about the Apple Jacks, btw. To my colleagues at the Estipona Group and my clients, thank you for making my day job so fun, interesting, and challenging that I'm perfectly willing to stay up until 3 a.m. writing. To the Reno Foodies Facebook group, thank you for the fabulous suggestions—you guys know your stuff. To Ben McDonald from

• •

the Reno-Sparks Convention and Visitors Authority, thank you for putting in a good word for me with Reedy Press—and Southwest Spirit before that! I owe you lunch or a billion dollars or something like that. To my Facebook friends, every single one, thank you for enduring my crowdsource requests, for giving feedback, and for always providing warm words of support. I only wish I could name you all individually, but alas, my publisher said "nope."

And finally, dear reader, whoever you are: Thank *you*.

• •

FOOD AND DRINK

MEET 'EM HALFWAY
AT CASALE'S HALFWAY CLUB

If there is an iconic, truly Reno experience, you'll find it at Casale's Halfway Club, which opened its doors in 1937. As unpretentious as it is rich in history, you'll want to spend time soaking up home-style history with owner "Mama" Inez Stempeck or any of the staff, most of whom are from the Casale clan.

On any given day you might still find ninety-year-old Mama Inez in the kitchen, making traditional, hand-made, family recipes her mother brought directly from Italy. Mama's son Tony, who bartends and cooks, may even take you to the back room to show you original pasta presses from the 1920s.

Don't expect finery here, but do expect to leave feeling like you just spent the evening with your new favorite family—one that cooks the finest lasagna, ravioli, and spaghetti you'll ever taste.

2501 E 4th St., 775-323-3979
(reservations recommended)

GET "ROASTED"
AT THE SPARKS NUGGET OYSTER BAR

A wall of welcoming, aromatic steam will likely greet you as you enter the Oyster Bar, thanks to a series of specialty steam pots sitting atop the centerpiece bar, percolating the restaurant's signature dish. It's all about the pan roast at the Oyster Bar, but promise yourself you won't count your calories while you're there; heavy cream, butter, and decadent crab, lobster, shrimp, and oysters are the key ingredients.

The establishment is best known for its indulgent pan roast—which can be ordered featuring any of the above seafood choices or a combination of them all—but don't miss a Caesar salad while you're there, as the Nugget's famous dressing is also a highlight.

1100 Nugget Ave.
775-356-3300 or 800-648-1177
nuggetcasinoresort.com/dining-en.html

HAVE SECONDS, THIRDS, AND TWELFTHS
AT ALL-YOU-CAN-EAT SUSHI

If one hand roll is good, then two are better, right? Thus is the recipe for some of the best dining options in the Reno area, where most sushi bars offer all-you-can-eat experiences.

Eating sushi is the new black in the area, with sushi bars with different themes and specialties popping up in every corner of the city. Sit at the bar in these versatile establishments, strike up a conversation with the sushi chef, and he'll likely "help" you by offering his own favorites based on your tastes and preferences. And some of them will take you well outside of your comfort zone.

Resistance to the Reno sushi trend is futile; bring your appetite, your ninja chopstick skills, and be prepared for anything—and a little bit of everything.

A few faves:

Sushi Minato, 6795 S Virginia St., 775-870-1860

Tha Joint Sushi & Grill, 222 Los Altos Pkwy., Sparks, 775-626-8677
thajointsushi.com

2 Tha Joint Sushi & Grill, 160 W Plumb Ln., 775-870-9288
thajointsushi.com

TAKE A (WINE) WALK
ON THE WILD SIDE

The third Saturday of every month finds locals and tourists alike in downtown Reno on an epic treasure hunt of sorts. But instead of compasses, they'll carry wine glasses, and instead of gold and silver, they'll be hunting whites and reds.

The Reno Riverwalk District Wine Walk allows these treasure hunters to explore establishments along the Riverwalk, which lines the Truckee River near the southern end of downtown. They'll be in search of sips of wine to be added to their traveling wine glasses, purchased in any of the participating shops/stops, exploring the eclectic shops and businesses by way of a map of participating merchants.

The Reno Wine Walk offers participants the chance to discover new favorite haunts along the Truckee and neighboring streets in downtown Reno while imbibing with friends and family. And you do so with a heaping side of philanthropy, as the $20 wine-tasting ticket fee benefits local charities. Cheers!

Riverwalk District (lining the Truckee River in downtown Reno)
775-825-WALK (9255)
renoriver.org/features/wine-walk

"BASQUE" IN THE GLOW
OF A PICON PUNCH

Northern Nevada is renowned for its Basque heritage, as waves of immigrants in the American West turned to sheepherding in the region when they failed to get rich in the Gold Rush. So it makes perfect sense that one local beverage highlight pays culinary homage to this history. And while soups, slabs of meet, and abundant fries are always on the informal, family-friendly tables of the region's abundant Basque establishments, the before-and-after-dinner highlight can be ordered at the bar: Picon punch.

Known to some as the "Basque cocktail," the "punch" (which is definitely not in the same vein as Hi-C) is usually made with grenadine, club soda, a float of brandy, and some variant of Amer Picon, a hard-to-find bittersweet French liqueur with a unique nutty orange flavor. A word of warning: stop at two, unless you're interested in being "punch" drunk.

Louis' Basque Corner, 301 E 4th St., 775-323-7203
louisbasquecorner.com

Santa Fe Hotel, 235 Lake St., 775-323-1891

J T Basque Bar & Dining Room, 1426 US-395, Gardnerville
775-782-2074, jtbasquenv.com

ENJOY A SMALL (OR BIG) PLATE
AT TWISTED FORK

In south Reno, bordering a suburban enclave known as Damonte Ranch, sits a fairly traditional-looking restaurant that features food that is anything but. Its quirky name provides a glimpse into the theoretical underpinnings of the food, an almost Alice-Through-the-Looking-Glass world of Latin-influenced, uber-creative dishes.

The Twisted Fork is a local haunt known most for its seasonal array of stunning, scrumptious small plates. Perennial favorites include the tiger shrimp tamal, ceviche de atun, and short rib arepa. Sandwiches, burgers, and entrees round out the menu, but be sure you save room for dessert. That dark but decadent rabbit hole includes recent offerings like black cherry ricotta cheesecake with a tangy organic blackberry coulis, orange crème fraîche, and blood orange sorbet.

It's a wonderland, indeed.

1191 Steamboat Pkwy. #1400, 775-853-6033
twistedforkreno.com

SAY "HOLA" TO A MARGARITA
AT LOS COMPADRES

Maybe the best aspect of a margarita is its lacking seasonality; whether it's one hundred degrees outside or a driving snow storm, the flavorful drink is the perfect complement to homemade Mexican food. And perhaps the best margarita in town is served up at Los Compadres, a family-owned restaurant with a complementary family vibe.

Belly up to the bar on any evening, and you might see a crew of regulars playing dice and imbibing. Guests come for the sangria—which is rich in flavors and seems to have proprietary ingredients that elevate the flavor. But margaritas are the signature specialty, with just the right combination (and just enough alcohol—never watery, never bland).

Tomás is one of the joint's best bartenders. Begin a conversation with him, and he might jokingly say, "You can call me 'Honey' after your second margarita." Perhaps needless to say, Honey makes exceptional margaritas.

Sparks, 1250 Disc Dr., 775-800-1822
Downtown Reno, 1490 E 4th St., 775-786-9966
South Meadows, 25 Foothill Rd., 775-284-1301
loscompadresreno.com

REVEL IN HISTORY
AT THE CONEY ISLAND

"The Coney" has been a local institution for almost a century, owing to its early roots as a tamale factory in the business's first iteration in the 1920s. It then evolved into a restaurant in 1945 and has been continuously owned and operated by three generations of the Galletti family.

Heritage is evident throughout this Sparks landmark, but such no-frills dining usually invites abundant locals, many of whom have been making return trips for decades. The restaurant is open six days a week for lunch, with rotating specialties, but the time to see (and be seen) is during its weekly Wednesday dinner service, at 6:00 or 7:30. There you'll enjoy a homemade meal with multiple courses, all based on hearty family recipes.

Oh, and speaking of family: some locals even call it "Galletti's," but don't get confused. It's all the same historical, happy place for food and fun.

2644 Prater Way, Sparks, 775-358-6485
coneyislandbar.net

INDULGE IN A HASHTAG-WORTHY #NOTACRONUT
AT ROUNDS BAKERY

Rounds perhaps made its name on controversy, but its legacy resides in the yum. As the story goes, one of the bakery's signature offerings—a croissant-like donut—got the attention of a famous New York pastry chef, the inventor (and trademarker) of the "cronut." He ordered Rounds to cease and desist calling its pastries "cronuts," so Rounds' social media–savvy leadership took to Twitter and started a snarky, tongue-in-cheek apology campaign about its "#NotACronut."

The name stuck, and the #NotACronut remains the signature specialty at Rounds. They come filled or unfilled; one popular filled option is the Fancy Nancy—Nutella cream, toasted hazelnuts, chocolate drizzle, and coarse sea salt. But don't miss out on bagels (boiled then baked, pretty close to New Yorker standards), sandwiches, and salads. Just be sure you arrive early for the best pastry selections.

294 E Moana Ln., 775-329-0800
roundsbakery.com

TAKE A TRIP
TO TUSCANY (IN RENO) AT CALAFURIA

An open and airy remodeled home with clean lines and heavenly aromas is the setting of Calafuria, an up-and-coming regional destination for authentic Tuscan cuisine.

And "authentic" is the key word, as the restaurant opens its doors five days a week from 4:30 to 5:30 p.m. with its Aperitivo menu, a selection of drinks, wines, and snacks—think breads, locally sourced almonds, and olives—to be enjoyed right before dinner, just like in Italy.

Dinner is then served from 5:30 p.m. The tasting menu is impeccable and intended for whole-table dining, with its selection of appetizers and entrees, with dessert included. Or go with à la carte selections and choose from creative and traditional Tuscan takes on pasta, poultry, fish, and more.

725 S Center St., 775-360-5175
calafuriareno.com

HONE YOUR "CRAFT"
AT A LOCAL BREWERY

A large and growing home-brew culture in Reno is likely the launching pad for the region's recent influx of new distilleries, brewpubs, tap houses, and growler stations. The beer scene in Reno is thriving, attracting attention from national and even international industry experts. And the vibe in these locales is as distinct as the flavors—whether you're searching for an industrial space with exposed beams or a thriving bar atmosphere with exceptional pub fare, there's something for everyone in the Biggest Little City.

Nevada's state legislature only legalized brewpubs in 1993 (interesting considering gaming has been legal for far longer), but since then, production and interest have created opportunities for eternal hoppy-ness.

Be on the lookout for Reno Craft Beer Week, an annual event celebrating craft brews and sponsored by northern Nevada pubs and breweries.

BREWERIES TO TRY

Brasserie St. James
901 S Center St., 775-348-8888
brasseriesaintjames.com

Great Basin Brewery
846 Victorian Ave., Sparks
5525 S Virginia St., Reno
greatbasinbrewingco.com

IMBĪB Custom Brews
785 E 2nd St., 775-470-5996
imbibreno.com

Pigeon Head
840 E 5th St., 775-276-6766
pigeonheadbrewery.com

Silver Peak
124 Wonder St. and 135 N Sierra St.
silverpeakbrewery.com

The Brewer's Cabinet
475 S Arlington Ave., 775-348-7481
thebrewerscabinet.com

The Depot Craft Brewery Distillery
325 E 4th St., 775-737-4330
thedepotreno.com

HELP A HANGOVER
WITH AN AWFUL AWFUL
AT THE LITTLE NUGGET

There's a special kind of burger that Reno locals crave. And as it turns out, it's best consumed about 2 a.m., perhaps after a night of pub crawling or partying with friends. And it's only steps away from the Reno arch.

The Awful Awful is the local iconic hangover burger, and it can be found at the 24-hour Little Nugget. The small diner is the consummate "greasy spoon," an atmosphere that is only amplified by its proximity to an old-time Reno casino. But the burger is the main draw here; look around and you'll see almost everyone enjoying the burger—which was featured on the Travel Channel *Food Wars*—alongside a massive heaping of seasoned fries.

The biscuits and gravy are a must-try as well. If greasy burgers and biscuits and gravy won't cure what ails ya, we don't know what will.

233 N Virginia St., 775-323-0716

GO OFF THE EATEN PATH
WITH RENO FOOD TOURS

What do you get when you combine a heaping helping of history with a massive side of tempting food? Reno Food Tours, of course—a cultural and culinary tour company specializing in downtown and midtown Reno. These guided walking food tours are led by culinary storytellers, locals who have so much passion for the region, you can practically taste it.

On these tours, you'll explore neighborhoods and discover fascinating historic and architectural details, as well as learn about local food. Tours feature tastings at local restaurants, Q&As with chefs, and time spent learning about the best food and drink Reno has to offer.

P.S. A gift certificate is an amazing gift for a local or a soon-to-be visitor.

775-501-9293
renofoodwalks.com

DRINK IN THE ATMOSPHERE
AT DEATH & TAXES AND 1864

Craft cocktails—with their characteristic house-made syrups, small batch bitters and custom glassware—are sexy right now. And two locations in Reno have that craft-cocktail sexy vibe practically perfected.

Death & Taxes is a dark and intimate cocktail lounge specializing in fresh artisanal cocktails made with seasonal ingredients, house-made syrups, and infusions. Perhaps even more fun: they offer classes where you can learn mixology techniques or take a deep dive into the worlds of agave and bourbon, among other topics.

1864 is a corner bar awash in Victorian-style accouterments. You can collapse in one of many velvet fainting couches, sipping a lavender lemon drop, in the shadow of a portrait of President Lincoln—who was instrumental in making Nevada a state. Hello, 1864: the Civil War called, and it wants its bar back.

Death & Taxes Provisions and Spirits, 26 Cheney St., 775-324-2630
deathandtaxesreno.com

1864 Tavern, 290 California Ave., 775-329-1864
1864tavern.com

LET OFF SOME STEAM
AT THE DEPOT

Proving that everything old is new again, The Depot in downtown Reno began its eclectic life as the headquarters for the Nevada-California-Oregon Railroad in 1910. And while its current incarnation won't attract ticket-seeking passengers, it has proven to be just the ticket for locals looking for historic charm, craft beers, and unusual approaches to American cuisine.

The architects and designers stayed true to the building's roots, paying tribute to its storied past by keeping original architectural elements. And within this unique space, they also brew beer and distill their own rye and bourbon—with local ingredients to boot.

Add in a diverse pub fare menu featuring dinners, sandwiches, and killer snacks (mac and cheese bites topped with crab—'nuff said), and you've got the recipe for the coolest place in town.

325 E 4th St., 775-737-4330
thedepotreno.com

DINE IN STYLE
AT ZOZO'S RISTORANTE

A strip mall in Reno is hardly the place you'd expect to run taste-first into Old World Italy, but that's exactly what you'll find at Zozo's Ristorante. The exposed brick-lined walls, red-and-white checkered tablecloths, and grapevine-and-latticework ceiling provide the dazzling backdrop to a delightful culinary experience.

Owners Sid and Judy Ashton are practically omnipresent, one or the other often sitting at the small bar delivering fishbowl-sized glasses of wine to friends and patrons. Abundant, charming staff seems to magically refill baskets of mouthwatering garlic bread. And the menu reveals Italian fare that is both elegant and diverse, saucy and cheesy.

The location is small, so reservations are in order. And desserts are legendary—don't you dare skip the tiramisu.

3446 Lakeside Dr., 775-829-9449
zozosreno.com

TIP

While it doesn't grace the menu, an almost-nightly special at Zozo's is its signature seafood cioppino. The seafood changes seasonally but often includes clams, mussels, scallops, prawns, whitefish, and rock shrimp, all of which are served in a spicy red sauce over perfectly prepared pasta. A serving of succulent cioppino, Dean Martin crooning in the background, and the glittering white lights above will all serve to make you feel like you've stepped out of Reno and into a beautiful Italian café in New York City.
Ciao bella!

SKIP THE SILVERWARE
IN FAVOR OF FINGERS
AT ZAGOL'S ETHIOPIAN

Reno's first (and only) Ethiopian restaurant brings African traditions to the American West. But if you've never tried Ethiopian cuisine, don't be shy at Zagol: your wait staff will happily educate you on the finer art of the dining experience, which includes using just *injera*, a spongy Ethiopian flatbread made from teff flour, to scoop food—no silverware necessary!

Dining at Zagol is an experience to be savored, so spend some time with a few glasses of honey wine and a mouthwatering meal of exotically spiced beef, chicken, lamb, or vegetables, and top it all off with some fresh-brewed Ethiopian coffee.

Oh, and just in case you're reluctant: silverware is also available upon request. But what fun is that?

855 E 4th St., 775-786-9020
zagolofreno.com

JUMP IN THE LINE
DURING FOOD TRUCK EVENTS

Reno has a bustling food truck scene, but keep in mind the allure of food truck culture: it's hit and miss and often involves standing in lines, but it typically serves up incredible food. Avoid the need to ride around town in search of your dinner by visiting one of Reno's two best food truck experiences: Food Truck Fridays, produced by Reno Street Food, and Feed the Camel.

Food Truck Friday brings about thirty food, dessert, and drink vendors to Idlewild Park every Friday night in summer. It is one of the nation's top ten largest weekly food truck events.

Feed the Camel happens seasonally on Wednesday nights under the Keystone Bridge at the McKinley Arts and Culture Center. This is a food truck event combined with an arts bazaar.

Idlewild Park, 1900 Idlewild Dr., 775-825-2665
facebook.com/renostreetfood

McKinley Arts and Culture Center, 925 Riverside Dr., 775-450-0062
twitter.com/FeedTheCamel

DRINK IN THE VIEWS
AT LA VECCHIA

The evening sky in Reno is epic—not only do we have one of the most colorful neon skylines in the country, but we also have surrounding mountains that do their own vibrant dance as the sun sets. And perhaps nowhere in Reno can you dine and enjoy a more spectacular vantage point to watch this show than La Vecchia Ristorante.

Billed as modern Italian comfort food, the menu features homemade pasta, ravioli, and daily chef's specials. Italian born and trained, Chef Alberto Gazzola brings the tastes of northern Italy directly to the table for lunch or dinner.

So sit on the patio if weather permits or request a window table indoors, because the competition for your attention will be fierce between the succulent flavors on your plate and the stunning views beyond.

Oh, and they have an amazing bar. That, too.

3005 Skyline Blvd. #160, 775-825-1113
lavecchiareno.com

GET HAPPY DURING SOCIAL HOUR
AT BISTRO NAPA HAPPY HOUR

On any given day as the hour approaches 4 p.m. on the second floor of the Atlantis Casino Resort, you'll see enthusiastic wannabe diners waiting in clusters outside the gates of Bistro Napa restaurant. For the uninitiated, you may not know to arrive early: seats fill up fast when those gates swing open at 4 p.m.

Once seated, you'll be handed a menu, thus commencing the "happy" part of this experience: every small plate, signature cocktail, and drink listed is half off from 4 p.m. to 6 p.m. From baby artichokes to "sexy fries" (blanketed in Parmigiano Reggiano, white truffle oil, and fresh herbs), from ahi to wood-fired flatbreads, this is one of the best ways to sample small plates in this upscale California cuisine-style restaurant.

Atlantis Casino Resort Spa, 3800 S Virginia St., 775-335-4539
atlantiscasino.com/reno-restaurants/bistro-napa

BAKE HOPE INTO YOUR PIE
AT SMILING WITH HOPE PIZZA

Who knew pizza could be topped with mozzarella, pepperoni, and goodwill? Such is the premise underscoring Smiling with Hope Pizza, where owner Walter Gloshinski is introducing New York-style pizza made and served with love by locals, many of whom have developmental disabilities. Giving people with special needs hands-on work experiences is the goal, and tasty pizza pies, calzones, and cannoli are the mouthwatering byproduct.

Smiling with Hope is reminiscent of authentic small family pizzerias and Italian cafés. Tradition is part of the prep work, as the pies are baked in 1960s gas deck ovens—the gold standard for traditional New York pizza.

Go for the food, including some of the world's best garlic knots. Go for the experience, as happiness seems sprinkled on every item coming from the kitchen. And go for the hope. It's an unforgettable experience.

6135 Lakeside Dr. #101, 775-825-1070
smilingwithhopepizza.com

DISH ABOUT EXCEPTIONAL FOOD
AT DISH CAFÉ

Blink and you might miss the entrance to Dish Café, which is tucked in the corner of a nondescript building. But missing a Dish experience would be a crime, as the small and locally owned destination turns out some of the region's best sandwiches, soups, and salads.

Owners Nancy and Joe Horn bring humanity and wholesomeness to exquisite food throughout their menu offerings, focusing on locally sourced ingredients, antibiotic-, hormone-, and cruelty-free meats, and local free-range eggs. Guy Fieri agrees this is a local find, as he featured Dish on a 2010 episode of *Diners, Drive-ins and Dives* on Food Network.

Need a recommendation? A smoked turkey sandwich— Applegate Farms turkey, whipped cream cheese, organic tart cherry jam, and spinach—served on apple cinnamon swirl bread is like a lunch and dessert mash-up. You're welcome.

855 Mill St., 775-348-8264
dishcafecatering.com

GO BANANAS
AT WESTERN VILLAGE STEAKHOUSE

Western Village is a casino hotel with quite the local following; the main draw, however, is definitely not the property's bellowing slot machines or glittering lights, but rather the property's steakhouse.

White linen tablecloths are standard, and once seated, it's easy to forget you're inside a clamoring casino. Tableside salad preparation, indulgent appetizers, and steaks that melt in your mouth all grace the expansive menu.

And whatever you do, if you're a fan of the art form that is dessert: request the tableside preparation of bananas foster.

Such elegant flourishes might lead you to believe the bill will break the bank, but that's all part of the charm. The Western Village Steakhouse really is surprisingly affordable.

815 Nichols Blvd., Sparks, 775-353-4916
westernvillagesparks.com/dining/the-steak-house

FIND FOODIE "EDEN"
AT GREAT FULL GARDENS

If you're looking for a dining destination where eating will make you feel good about yourself, look no further than Great Full Gardens. The name itself implies the benefits: you'll eat many of these beautiful dishes with your eyes first, plus the restaurant's staff has made popular dietary choices like paleo, gluten-free, vegan, organic, GMO-free, and sustainable both mouthwatering and accessible.

They're open for breakfast, lunch, and dinner, meaning you can satisfy your cravings for tasty kale (it really does exist!) or a vegan "neatball" sandwich pretty much any time.

But if you're in the mood for some torture after a healthy meal, try the aptly named J'aime Tortue Liege Waffle: toasted pecans over salted caramel ice cream in a web of chocolate and caramel sauces, all atop a caramelized Liège waffle.

After all, the first course was healthy.

Great Full Gardens Midtown
555 S Virginia St., 775-324-2013

Great Full Gardens Express/Joe Crowley Student Union
1664 N Virginia St., 775-682-9590

Great Full Gardens South Meadows
748 South Meadows Blvd. A14, 775-324-2016
greatfullgardens.com

YOU'LL BE SHOUTING "BLOODY GOOD"
AFTER THESE LOCAL BLOODY MARY CHOICES

Reno is perhaps better known for its craft beer and cocktail reputation than for Bloody Marys, but per capita, you'd be hard pressed to find a better menu of exceptional options than locally. Some are more "breakfast" and less "drink," containing bacon, shrimp, beef sticks, pickled eggs—really, the sky is the limit. And many also use locally distilled liquor, which just adds to the homegrown flavor.

So the best recommendation is this: decide what area of town you're visiting (Virginia City? Midtown? Truckee?), pick a bar or restaurant, and strap in for a wild ride. And look for the characteristic touches that make these Bloody Marys bloody better, like the jalapeño vodka used at Brewers Cabinet or Stone House's Bloody Maria, made with jalapeño-infused tequila and homemade Mary mix.

BLOODY MARYS

Bar of America
10040 Donner Pass Rd., Truckee, CA, 530-587-2626
barofamerica.com

Brewers Cabinet
475 S Arlington Ave., 775-348-7481
thebrewerscabinet.com

Bucket of Blood
1 South C St., Virginia City, 775-847-0322
bucketofbloodsaloon.com

Stone House
1907 S Arlington Ave., 775-284-3895
stonehousecafereno.com

The Depot Craft Brewery Distillery
325 E 4th St., 775-737-4330
thedepotreno.com

DINE HERE
TO FIND YOUR INNER RAPSCALLION

You'll feel like you've stepped out of the 21st century and into Old World San Francisco when you walk through the doors of Rapscallion, a Reno seafood institution. And the food reflects this old-school ambiance combined with a contemporary twist, with twenty varieties of fresh fish daily—likely placing it among the most prolific Reno restaurants for fresh fish offerings.

Dinners are upscale and sophisticated, whereas lunches are a bit more casual. But the dark wood surroundings, dim lights, and linen tablecloths are present no matter what time you're dining. And the expansive mahogany bar attracts visitors who range from vintage to hipster and everywhere in between.

Hint: Rapscallion's Linguini and Fresh Manilla Clams with house-made clam sauce is unparalleled; finish your meal with flourless chocolate truffle cake for the ultimate old-school experience.

1555 S Wells Ave., 775-323-1211
rapscallion.com

CAMP OUT AT CAMPO

Rustic neighborhood charm is the name of the game at Campo, whether you're at the Reno or Sparks location. Executive Chef David Holman is bringing his own flair to a much-loved, established restaurant that has a reputation for creativity and connection.

The menu highlights local ingredients from regional farms and ranches, perhaps best illustrated by the D.R.O.P.P. Salad— Distributors of Regional Organic Produce and Products. The salad's components change daily, but rest assured, you're getting the brightest flavors from seasonal selections.

Also popular are Napoletana-style pizzas fired in Campo's wood-burning oven, handmade pastas, and house-made salumi. But if available, tried-and-true favorites like roasted brussels sprouts, wood-fired cauliflower, and Campo's signature kale salad with poached egg, lemon-garlic vinaigrette, and crispy Grana Padano are sure to please.

Campo Reno
50 N Sierra St., 775-737-9555

Campo Sparks
137 Los Altos Pkwy., Sparks, 775-501-8970
camporeno.com

CRAWL, DON'T RUN,
TO AREA BARS AND PUBS

To say Reno has a "reputation" is a good thing—as long as that reputation includes safe, quirky, and fun special events and gatherings. And of late, we've earned a certain reputation for hosting the best beer crawls in the country.

Almost every month of the year while you're wandering around downtown Reno or Sparks, you might bump into groups of Santas, leprechauns, zombies, cowboys, or pirates—depending on the season.

Most crawls will offer points at which you can buy a glass, get a map, don your wristband, and then be eligible for discounts on refills at a variety of pubs and bars. It's a good way to explore the local bar scene—while dressed in your finest costumes.

Because everything is better—even drinking—while dressed like a superhero.

newtoreno.com/reno-beer-crawls.htm

ENJOY COFFEE, TEA, OR VINO
AT LOCAL HOTSPOTS

Craving some caffeine? Or perhaps it's late in the day, and you're not quite sure if it's happy hour or sleepytime? We've got you covered.

Too Soul Tea Co., a locally owned teahouse, has the largest and finest loose leaf tea and blends available. The accommodating staff can help you pick the exact tea to satisfy your cravings—whether you need a pick-me-up, a calm-me-down, or an anywhere-in-between. They sell online and in their charming store in Midtown.

And what better complementary combination than a coffee shop that also sells wine? Or is it a wine bar that also sells coffee? Either way, Swill is awesome, offers great Wi-Fi with weekly changing passwords that will make you smile, and friendly service. They also have a life-changing spice chai latte.

Too Soul, 542 1/2 Plumas St., 775-322-2001
toosoultea.com

Swill, 3366 Lakeside Ct., 775-823-9876
swillreno.com

MUSIC AND ENTERTAINMENT

TAKE A TRIP DOWN MUSICAL MEMORY LANE
AT RECYCLED RECORDS

Sometimes, you just need some good old-fashioned vinyl. And in Reno, if you're craving the scratchy sounds of a turntable recording, Recycled Records is the place to find 'em. But the fun doesn't stop there: CDs (need to hear some Milli Vanilli or Springsteen?), cassettes (no mix tapes, but there's abundant fodder here), and even some eight-tracks and reel-to-reels can be found among the many treasures.

They'll even buy from and/or trade with you. Just in case you still have a shoebox full of ancient gems.

As the name implies, it's a secondhand retail music store, but what the name doesn't reveal is the store's longevity: it's been a go-to destination for music lovers since 1978. The staff is knowledgeable, the store has a natural funky vibe, and the smell? Well, it's a lot like teen spirit.

822 S Virginia St., 775-826-4119
recrecreno.com

HUM TO THE RHYTHM OF THE RIVER
AT SIERRA WATER GARDENS

Sure, this is a boutique specialty nursery that sells super-cool things like koi, water plants, succulents, and air plants. And no, this entry is not misfiled in the "Music and Entertainment" category.

Because during summer months, Sierra Water Gardens transforms into the coolest music venue around—mostly bluegrass and almost always homegrown. Bring a low-back chair, some wine, and a picnic basket full of cheeses, olives, and crackers, and watch as musical guests grace the gardens' "back porch" stage and bring you their raw music, pure and magical.

The tranquil setting—with the trickling Truckee River bordering the property—enhances the organic vibe. Entertainment usually happens on weekends from around April to September, depending on the weather.

2110 Dickerson Rd., 775-622-4090
sierrawatergardens.com

WALK ON WATER
AT LEX NIGHTCLUB

Reno typically rejects comparisons to Las Vegas, but there's one destination that perhaps rivals even the splashiest offered by our shiny sister down south: LEX Nightclub, tucked inside the Grand Sierra Resort. Once inside this nightlife venue, you're greeted by a sea of skin, screens, scaffolding, and glowsticks, as popular DJs and Grammy-winning acts ignite the stage.

Intricate skylights and a $2 million lighting system provide an impressive backdrop to the club's twenty-five-thousand square feet of space, highlighted by an indoor pool that is partially covered by a glass dance floor, creating the illusion of dancing on water.

LEX features three full bars, thirty-three VIP tables, and a VIP guest list. Keep in mind that the dress code is "upscale at management discretion," but make no mistake: this truly is a one-of-a-kind experience worthy of your upscale wardrobe.

Grand Sierra Resort and Casino, 2500 E 2nd St., 775-789-5399
lexnightclub.com

TAKE A TRIP TO ARTOWN
DURING THE MONTH OF JULY

When Artown began as an arts festival in 1996, it attracted thirty thousand guests to various arts and music events during a three-week period in July. Now, two decades later, attendance is more than three hundred thousand, and the festival spans the entire month.

Intended as a way to strengthen Reno's arts community, enhance our civic identity, and create a climate for the cultural and economic rebirth of our region, Artown now annually fills a calendar with nearly five hundred events, more than one hundred workshops, and more than thirty ongoing programs. Past performers like India.Arie, the Glenn Miller Orchestra, Mikhail Baryshnikov, UB40, and Michael Bublé have headlined, but you'll find something to do multiple times each day during the month of July. Workshops, dance, film, theater, and kids' programming are all part of the mix.

And best of all: most events are free or low cost.

775-322-1538
renoisartown.com

ENJOY A MIDSUMMER NIGHT'S DREAM
AT THE LAKE TAHOE SHAKESPEARE FESTIVAL

In terms of entertainment, one of the most unique experiences in the area involves late summer evenings, Shakespeare, lake views, stars, and sand. The Lake Tahoe Shakespeare Festival marries all of these concepts quite functionally, inviting audiences to watch the Bard's works play out on an outdoor stage resting along the shores of Lake Tahoe. The viewers, sitting in outdoor lounge chairs under blankets brought from home, can run their toes through the sand, sip a glass of wine, and chat with friends during intermission.

The acclaimed festival is usually raucous, always well attended, and abundantly fun. The natural sand amphitheater overlooking Lake Tahoe provides awe-inspiring views before the sun goes down, and after, actors on stage compete for your attention against the gorgeous starry skies above.

Bring a flashlight, dress in layers, and be prepared for a night of unparalleled views and Shakespearean fun.

Sand Harbor at Lake Tahoe State Park
2005 Highway 28, 1-800-747-4697
laketahoeshakespeare.com

SOAR TO NEW HEIGHTS
AT THE GREAT RENO BALLOON RACES

A mosaic of floating balloons is the paint and Reno skies are the canvas during the annual Great Reno Balloon Race, the largest free hot-air ballooning event in the world.

During three days in early September, you can look up at sunrise from just about any corner of the region to see about one hundred hot air balloons dotting the tranquil horizon. Many locals remember the event's humble beginnings in 1982, when just hundreds of spectators watched twenty balloons launch from Rancho San Rafael Park. But now, the Great Reno Balloon Race has taken flight with more balloons, more entertainment, and thousands more spectators.

Arrive pre-dawn for the stained-glass effect of Dawn Patrol and the Glow Show, bring some cocoa and blankets, and be prepared for the "Wow."

Rancho San Rafael Park
1595 N Sierra St., 775-826-1181
renoballoon.com

CATCH A SHOW
AT BARTLEY RANCH

Any chance you get to watch a performance in Bartley Ranch, take it: the Robert Z. Hawkins Amphitheater is a uniquely northern Nevada venue with an intimate open-air atmosphere ideal for taking in stage performances under summer skies and the stars.

During summer months, the park calendar is chock full of performances. From plays and concerts to festivals, the facility hosts a little of everything. The amphitheater is built into a hillside and accommodates about one thousand of your closest friends and family—either in seats or on blankets atop a grassy slope.

While there, check out the historic Huffaker Schoolhouse, built in 1867, which can also be rented out for performances and weddings.

6000 Bartley Ranch Rd.
washoecounty.us/parks/specialty_facilities/hawkins_amphitheater.php

GET TO KNOW THE "GOLDEN TURTLE":
RENO'S PIONEER CENTER

If you're traveling down Virginia Street heading south from downtown, you can't miss a golden, somewhat retro-looking dome. Under this roof is Reno's Pioneer Center for the Performing Arts, which was built in 1967, its gold-anodized aluminum geodesic dome comprised of five hundred panels glistening in the sun. Inside, the orchestra level of the theater is depressed below ground level, allowing the roof to nearly touch the ground at the corners.

Locals lovingly refer to the building, which was named to the National Register of Historic Places in 2005, as the "golden turtle."

The building then and now is one of Reno's iconic cultural touchstones, with frequent appearances by the Reno Chamber Orchestra, Reno Philharmonic, and A.V.A. Ballet Theatre. It also is home to Broadway Comes to Reno, which has been bringing touring Broadway shows to Reno for decades.

100 S Virginia St., 775-686-6600 or tickets by phone: 1-866-553-6605
pioneercenter.com

EXPLORE YOUR SPIRITUAL SIDE
IN LOCAL CHURCHES

Music and religion often go hand in hand, so it makes sense that some of the region's most poignant musical experiences take place in local churches.

Overlooking the Truckee River downtown is Trinity Episcopal Church, built in the 1920s. The church is known for its musical gifts to the community—namely a 32-bell carillon, as well as a Casavant Frères pipe organ with its 37 ranks and 2,177 pipes. Trinity offers free organ concerts and recitals featuring local and regional organists. Be prepared to "feel" the music as the pipe organ bellows and sings.

Another fascinating spiritual experience featuring abundant music can be found on a hilltop overlooking Reno and the valley beyond. This is Carmel of Reno, a monastery for Carmelite nuns. Music is part and parcel to their experience, and the public is invited to join the nuns for prayer and mass.

Trinity Episcopal Church, 200 Island Ave., 775-329-4279
trinityreno.org

Carmel of Reno, 1950 La Fond Dr., 775-323-3236
carmelofreno.com

TIP

When you think of nuns, you may not immediately think of technology; but Sister Claire Sokol of Carmel of Reno recently used technology to unite more than one hundred Carmelite voices from twenty-three countries in a virtual choir, a moving piece that marks the 500th Anniversary of Saint Teresa's birth. Sister Claire's music, combined with technology, allowed these nuns—many of whom don't venture outside of cloistered spaces—to unify without ever having to leave their monasteries. Watch an award-winning documentary about the making of the virtual choirs, produced by Reno's KNPB, at knpb.org/virtualharmony.

Experience the virtual choirs at youtube.com/user/ STJ500virtualchoirs.

DON'T BREAK A LEG
IN ONE OF RENO'S MANY THEATERS

Reno's theater scene is scrappy, undeniable, and fierce. And all of these indomitable characteristics are in full display at many local theaters, including Reno Little Theater, Brüka, and Good Luck Macbeth.

Reno Little Theater is tucked away in the bungalow district known as West of Wells. It's Nevada's longest-running community theater and features musicals, comedy, mystery, suspense, and drama. Performances are frequently sold out, so get your tickets early. And don't miss the monthly Sunday jazz shows, featuring many of the most prominent musicians in the Reno jazz scene.

Brüka Theatre is a performance art space in the downtown core devoted to classic, contemporary, musical, original, and children's theater.

Good Luck Macbeth, as the name implies, is known for Shakespeare, but it also offers original pieces, blood-filled Halloween extravaganzas, and classical productions.

Reno Little Theater, 147 E Pueblo St., 775-329-0661
renolittletheater.org

Brüka, 99 N Virginia St., 775-323-3221
bruka.org

Good Luck Macbeth, 713 S Virginia St., 775-322-3716
goodluckmacbeth.org

LOL AT RENO-TAHOE COMEDY
AT THE PIONEER UNDERGROUND

The "golden turtle" is the venue (page 43), or at least the stairs in front behind the statue leading subterranean will deliver you to the venue. This quirky location (treasure map not provided) frames the experience: it's a fairly compact setting with theater seats and a low ceiling, but the intimacy makes the laughter that much more contagious.

Many of the comedians featured in the experience are regulars in the industry—Showtime, HBO, Comedy Central, and syndicated radio shows are their other comedy homes.

Be sure to take advantage of reduced ticket prices for advance purchases.

100 S Virginia St., 775-322-5233
renotahoecomedy.com

BECOME A GROUPIE
FOR LOCAL BANDS

Music is rising up from the underground in the Biggest Little City, and many bands have strong local roots (even if they frequently tour around greener pastures). All of these groups either call Reno their permanent home or come back often to play in local venues, including Studio on 4th, the Holland Project, Jub Jub's Thirst Parlor, the Saint, and more.

If you get a chance to experience any of these, count yourself lucky; we expect great things to happen for these (and many more) as Reno's music scene continues to explode.

LOCAL BANDS

Jelly Bread: rock, roots, funk, soul
jellybread.net

Mel Wade: acoustic and bluesy-folk soul
reverbnation.com/melwade

Moondog Matinee: rock, blues, indie
moondogmatinee.com

Schizopolitans: cinematic, avant-rock
schizopolitans.bandcamp.com

Sierra Sweethearts: bluegrass, swing, doo-wop,
folk, and a lot of silly
sierrasweethearts.com

The Novelists: lyrical rock
thenovelists.com

Wheatstone Bridge: American folk
facebook.com/WheatstoneBridgeBand

ALL AGES ARE INVITED
TO THE HOLLAND PROJECT

If you're looking to introduce a teenager or young adult to that distinctly Reno vibe, check out the Holland Project. This all-ages arts and music initiative by young people, for young people, usually hosts events a few nights a week during peak seasons.

The nonprofit project's goals are to provide art and music access, diverse workshop opportunities, and community involvement and collaboration. Lofty goals to be sure, but the incredibly friendly and supportive staff accomplishes this—and then some.

This small, chill venue emits an urban vibe and is welcome to people of all ages and hosts local bands—both veterans and new to the scene—as well as gallery exhibits and independent art events.

140 Vesta St., 775-742-1858
hollandreno.org

CHECK OUT RENO'S
COOLEST MUSIC VENUES

Looking for a destination to chill and enjoy some music? With Reno's growing music scene, more and more exciting venues are popping up. Here are just a few that deserve a visit.

Pignic invites you to bring your own uncooked dinner selection to this community grill for a carefree evening of grilling and chilling. Many evenings feature live entertainment in a range of genres. They also host open mic nights for aspiring artists.

The Saint features live performances and dance parties in an unusually intimate environment for a music venue—some free, some ticketed. Both emerging and national artists are drawn to the Saint's unique vibe and ambiance.

Pignic, 235 Flint St., 775-376-1948
facebook.com/pignicpub

The Saint Reno, 761 S Virginia St., 775-221-7451
thesaintreno.com

GROOVE TO THE SOUNDS OF CULTURE
AT THE NEVADA MUSEUM OF ART

While art is always part of music, music does not always accompany art. But it does in Reno twice a week, thanks to the Nevada Museum of Art. The cultural epicenter of downtown Reno brings together locals and visitors alike for two opportunities to swing to live music while exploring the latest exhibits.

First Thursday happens—big surprise—the first Thursday of each month from 5 p.m. to 7 p.m. There, you'll be able to grab a drink, groove to live and local music, then check out the museum's current exhibitions.

Then every weekend, the museum hosts Sunday Music Brunch from 10 a.m. to 2 p.m. These brunches, presented by chez louie, feature artful dishes, mimosas, and a Bloody Mary bar—with a healthy accompaniment of live music.

160 W Liberty St., 775-329-3333
nevadaart.org

SIP A MARTINI
AT ROXY'S

On the second level of the Eldorado Hotel Casino is an iconic, twenty-piece fountain—appropriately named the Fountain of Fortune, considering it's a casino. And overlooking that fountain is Roxy's Bar & Lounge.

How fortunate, indeed.

Roxy's Piano Bar is the place to be nightly, with its live piano and vocals that'll take you well into the morning hours. The music is either the reason you've come, or it's the ideal backdrop to the pièce de résistance: the drink in your hand. Roxy's is famous for its menu of 102 martinis and selection of 350 wines.

So sip a martini, bask in the glow of the Fountain of Fortune, and watch as the ivories are gloriously tickled in Roxy's Piano Bar.

Eldorado Resort Casino
345 N Virginia St., 775-786-5700
eldoradoreno.com/venue/restaurants/roxy

SPORTS, RECREATION, AND OUTDOOR ADVENTURE

CLIMB THE WALLS
AT WHITNEY PEAK'S BASECAMP

If you're looking for something to get the adrenaline pumping, consider a visit to Whitney Peak's BaseCamp. This destination is a celebration of climbing and fitness that occupies the entire second floor of the non-gaming, non-smoking boutique hotel in downtown Reno.

Rock walls, gymnast rings, a slackline, and a full gym are featured indoors. But the part of the experience that will keep you talking: the outdoor rock wall, which at 164 feet is the world's tallest artificial climbing wall.

Locals often challenge their guests to experience the best view of our iconic Reno arch: from the tippy-top of the wall. You'll literally be scaling a major hotel, in the heart of downtown Reno, above the city's main thoroughfare and most identifiable landmark.

No biggie.

255 N Virginia St., 775-398-5400 or 888-776-9551
whitneypeakhotel.com

SWING FOR THE FENCES
WITH SOME GOOD
OL' FASHIONED ACEBALL

Baseball season in northern Nevada is perhaps our favorite time of the year. On any given game day, you'll find us at the park, drinking a beer, watching our favorite team: the Reno Aces.

The Triple-A affiliate of the Arizona Diamondbacks plays at Greater Nevada Field in the heart of Reno, a destination that has spurred its own retail and nightlife neighborhood called the Freight House District. Watch a game, then visit one of the many surrounding bars and clubs for a taste of after-hours fun.

A few tips: don't try to guess what the mascot is (our best guess is a uvula, but the unknown is part of the charm); watch the scoreboard during the seventh-inning stretch; and aim to attend on a night offering fireworks, which usually happen on weekends.

Play ball!

Greater Nevada Field
250 Evans Ave., 775-334-7000
renoaces.com

PERFECT YOUR CAMEL SPIN
AT THE DOWNTOWN RENO ICE RINK

Winter months used to find the Greater Nevada Field, home to the Reno Aces, vacant; what better place to install a quaint ice rink? The City of Reno made that happen, and now the rink—which offers abundant free parking due to its proximity to the ballpark—is a popular destination for all ages.

With the towering buildings comprising downtown Reno's skyline in the background and the glow of the landmark baseball sculpture above and around, singles, pairs, and groups dance on ice. Prices are reasonable, and the surrounding Freight House District offers abundant options for beverages after—either the adult variety or those that are more kid-friendly.

So muster that courage, bundle up, and head downtown for some great fun at Reno's ice rink. Whether you're a novice or a pro, the ice doesn't care.

Greater Nevada Field
250 Evans Ave., 775-334-7035

SPEND A DAY
(OR NIGHTS)
AT THE RITZ AND NORTHSTAR

If you've ever wanted to visit the Ritz but perhaps can't quite justify an overnight stay, head up to the Ritz-Carlton Lake Tahoe for some Tahoe-style outdoor fun. Whether you've spent the day skiing Northstar (the ski resort adjacent to the Ritz) or hiking the surrounding trails during warmer months, guests gather around the fire pit in the evenings year-round to be schooled in the fine art of s'more-making, as taught by the property's resident marshmologist.

The outdoor terrace also features oversized board games, bocce, and ping pong. So grab a drink, play outdoors in the shadow of abundant tall pines, journey inside for dinner, and then return to your room. Or not. All visitors can take advantage of games and s'mores, complimentary.

The property also has a gondola that connects it to the Village at Northstar, where you can ice skate, shop, and play.

13031 Ritz-Carlton Highlands Ct., Truckee, CA, 530-562-3000
ritzcarlton.com/en/hotels/california/lake-tahoe

TAKE A HIKE
(OR 7 OR 23)

Northern Nevada's high-desert terrain makes the ideal landscape for hikers who enjoy rocks, sagebrush, evergreens, water features, and everything in between. It's practically impossible to mention all the incredible hiking trails in and around Reno, so here we'll note two local favorites: Galena and Hunter Creek Trail.

Galena Canyon, south of town, contains diverse trails for every aptitude level. About seven different nature trails comprise the well-mapped system, with brochures and signposts available to tell you about the ecology and cultural history of the area.

Hunter Creek Trail is more a locals' secret—or at least so lore suggests, though the trail can get very busy. Go early for the most solitude; also note that the trail is mostly in sun, which can be brutal in summer. However, the payoff, about three miles up, is superb: Hunter Creek Falls, bookended by rocky banks and verdant hillsides.

Galena Creek Visitor Center
six miles up Mt. Rose Hwy. from south Reno, 775-849-4948
galenacreekvisitorcenter.org/area-trails.html

Hunter Creek Trail
trailhead on Woodchuck Cir. in west Reno
alltrails.com/trail/us/nevada/hunter-creek-trail--2

TIP

So many trails, so little space
in this book—so here's a place you
can go to download and/or flip through a
comprehensive collection of trails in and around
the Truckee Meadows. This was compiled by
the cities of Reno and Sparks, as well as Washoe
County and the Reno-Sparks Convention and
Visitors Authority, so it provides a good 60-plus–
page overview of the elaborate trails available to
Reno hikers.
Go forth, download, and get hiking!

visitrenotahoe.com/reno-tahoe/what-to-do/
camp-rv/hiking-guide

HAVE A TUBE-ULAR EXPERIENCE
FLOATING THE TRUCKEE RIVER

A river runs through downtown Reno, meaning the view from the water can be spectacular. During months when the weather is warm and the Truckee River has enough water, tubing is a mostly relaxing adventure—with a little adrenaline thrown in for good measure. You'll see abundant changes in ecology as you float the cold water and even view a line of historic Reno mansions along the way.

And some companies, like Tahoe Whitewater Tours, will let you rent an inner tube, life jackets, and helmets, provide a safety orientation, and even give you an upstream lift in a shuttle.

From your upstream destination, it's between a two- and four-hour float back down to the Whitewater Park.

Tahoe Whitewater Tours, (530) 587-5777
gowhitewater.com/tubing-the-truckee-2

TIP

Rent an extra tube to carry your cooler for a picnic or beverages. Or both!

GO IN SEARCH OF WILD HORSES

Dotting the hillsides surrounding Reno—and oftentimes venturing into suburban neighborhoods—wild horses are abundant and revered in northern Nevada. To see a horse in the wild is an unforgettable experience, harkening back to images of the Wild West in centuries past. Many locations in and around town are hotbeds for wild horse sightings—from Damonte Ranch to Hidden Valley to the Virginia City foothills and beyond.

There's even a locally based company that provides tours, some to wild horse sanctuaries set at the foothills of the towering mountain ranges, others to Pyramid Lake or the Virginia Foothills.

Whichever you choose—wild or guided—take some time to explore the surrounding desert landscape to try to find a horse in the wild!

Sonny Boys Tours, 775-200-5205
renowildhorsetours.com

SHOUT "FORE" TO NUMBER 15
AT LAKERIDGE GOLF COURSE

Did you know that Reno and its surrounding communities are scientifically made for better golfing? Seriously. At our altitude, the Reno-Sparks Convention and Visitors Authority tells us, golf balls fly ten percent farther.

If that doesn't convince you to golf here, we don't know what will.

Within ninety minutes of Reno, you'll find more than fifty golf courses. So the choices are abundant. But local golfing lore is all about the 15th hole of LakeRidge Golf Course. One can only imagine what Robert Trent Jones, Sr., was thinking when he designed this hole, whose tee sits 145 feet above a 239-yard hole on a natural island green.

It's a world-famous par 3, and it's begging for you to conquer it.

LakeRidge Golf Course
1218 Golf Club Dr., 775-825-2200
duncangolfreno.com

GET STARSTRUCK
AT LAKE TAHOE

Light pollution makes stargazing in the Truckee Meadows difficult, but one only needs to head to the hills to find locations where the stars will spread before you like fireflies swarming in the night sky.

With clear skies happening about three hundred days per year in the area, Lake Tahoe proves the ultimate location for celestial viewing. So pack your telescope, binoculars, cocoa, and blankets, and check out these (among other) prime locations.

Slide Mountain
Mt. Rose-Ski Tahoe Winters Creek Lodge Parking Lot:
breathtaking views overlooking Washoe Lake

Nevada Beach
(U.S. Highway 50, Round Hill): endless open beach and sky views

Monitor Pass
(Highway 395, 2.5 miles south of the Nevada state line, then take Highway 89 west toward Markleeville): an overlook with dramatic sky and lake vistas

DISCOVER
TAHOE'S HIDDEN CASTLE: VIKINGSHOLM

In the mood to feel like Cinderella for a day? A steep one-mile hike that drops five hundred feet in elevation will make you glad you forgot your glass slippers. But at the end, you'll be standing on the shores of Emerald Bay at Lake Tahoe, admiring a magnificent "castle" that perfectly complements nature's surrounding beauty.

Vikingsholm is considered one of the finest examples of Scandinavian architecture in the United States, and most of the materials to construct the home came from the Tahoe Basin. The thirty-eight-room mansion is open for tours during the summer months.

Keep in mind, after touring the architectural marvel of Vikingsholm, you have a challenge ahead of you: a five-hundred-foot incline, rising to an elevation of sixty-three hundred feet, which means breathing is more labored. And sadly, no pumpkin carriages are available for transport.

Vikingsholm Castle via Vikingsholm parking lot
by Highway 89 at Emerald Bay
Tours provided by the Sierra State Parks Foundation, sierrastateparks.org

JOIN THE 165-MILE CLUB
ON THE TAHOE RIM TRAIL

When you have the Jewel of the Sierra in your backyard, might as well encircle it with vantage points from which one can observe and admire said jewel, right? The Tahoe Rim Trail is just that— 165 miles circling Lake Tahoe along the ridges and mountaintops of northern California and northern Nevada. It's maintained with mountain bikers, hikers, and equestrians in mind, though keep in mind there are places bikes can't access.

Obviously, you don't have to travel it all in one shot; the TRT has eight distinct sections, all reachable by major roads.

The trail took sixteen years to complete and winds through six counties, three national forests, and state park land. Conditions are best from mid-July through mid-September, so plan accordingly to witness some of the most spectacular views of the lake and surrounding peaks, forests, and meadows you'll ever find.

tahoerimtrail.org

CHANNEL YOUR INNER PHIL MICKELSON
AT THE GSR'S SIERRA BAY AQUA GOLF

Truth be told, the best aspect of this innovative driving range is that you don't have to be a pro to have fun. In fact, you don't even have to own clubs, considering rentals are available.

With scenic Mt. Rose in the distance, guests can put some "splash" back into their golf game by shooting for one of eight island greens of varying distance and difficulty, all on the Grand Sierra Resort's massive outdoor reservoir.

Golfers good enough to land a hole-in-one are rewarded with prizes, while those with room for improvement can receive instruction from on-hand PGA professionals.

Food and drink are available, but you can also BYOB. Meaning the GSR may just be your new BGFF—Best Golfing Friend Forever.

Grand Sierra Resort
2500 E 2nd St., 775-789-2122
grandsierraresort.com/activities/sierra-bay-aqua-golf

FOLLOW YOUR STREAM
OF CONSCIOUSNESS
ALONG THE TRUCKEE

While it's common for cities to literally "spring" from water, it's fairly uncommon for a river to as clearly define a region as the Truckee River defines our area. The river starts in Lake Tahoe, the Truckee being Tahoe's only significant outlet, and it travels downstream 121 miles to Pyramid Lake.

So an interesting journey is to follow the Truckee River, watching the changing environment along the way. It begins at Lake Tahoe Dam near Tahoe City and saunters from there through the quaint town of Truckee, which is only thirty minutes from Reno. From Truckee it mostly follows the I-80 corridor, turning sharply east to leave California and find its home in Nevada, meandering through Reno and Sparks. Ultimately, it winds up at stark and somewhat eerie Pyramid Lake, a remnant of prehistoric Lake Lahontan on the Pyramid Lake Indian Reservation.

A bikeway following the river is also under construction, called the Truckee-Pyramid Bikeway. Regardless of how you tackle it, what an incredible journey.

Truckee-Pyramid Bikeway, 775-825-9868
tpbikeway.org

KEEP YOUR EYES
ON THE SKIES

People who visit Reno are often struck by our clouds, which vary in size, texture, and density. This is all thanks to the Sierra Nevada, because as winds hit the range, air and moisture rise. This creates clouds that can resemble anything ranging from an alien invasion to Monet's pastel brushstrokes.

You don't even need to see the sun as it rises or sets to experience the majesty; the way dawn and dusk themselves change the textures and hues of the sky and the colors of the mountains are remarkable from pretty much any vantage point.

But here are a few local favorites:

- Rancho San Rafael Park, north Reno
- Emerald Bay, Lake Tahoe
- Pretty much any beach, Lake Tahoe
- Windy Hill, southwest Reno
- Donner Lake, CA
- The hills in east Sparks, notably on trails surrounding Wingfield Springs and Red Hawk

HOWL IN SUPPORT
OF THE NEVADA WOLF PACK

Reno is a college town through and through, which means you'll encounter rabid fans on game day, flying Wolf Pack flags, dressed in silver and blue, and battling for prime parking places around campus.

There's fun to be had at every meet, game, and competition—from catching baseball at Peccole Park to watching the Pack shoot hoops at Lawlor Events Center to cheering on a blitz in an intense clash over pigskin at Mackay Stadium, which sits high on the hill overlooking campus.

But that's not all, obviously. Regardless of the season, you'll likely find a sport and a game to watch—soccer, tennis, swim and dive, and many more. Attending a University of Nevada, Reno sports event is a uniquely northern Nevada experience, one that brings out the Pack Pride in all of us.

nevadawolfpack.com

TAKE A DEEP DIVE
INTO HISTORY AT BOWERS MANSION

Pack a picnic lunch and take a trip through time to the Victorian era at Bowers Mansion Regional Park, situated between Reno and Carson City in North Washoe Valley. The lush greens surrounding the mansion itself are perfect spots for a blanket and some quiet contemplative time, while the kids (and kids at heart) can soak up some fun in the pool.

Located right next to the historic mansion, this fun "Z"-shaped, forty-four-meter, outdoor pool is heated by a natural hot spring. A wading pool is also available for small children.

On the grounds, you'll find children's play areas and abundant places to explore—including a hiking trail leading to the Bowers family gravesite. You can also tour the mansion for a sneak peek into the life of the home's original owners, Comstock millionaires Eilley and Sandy Bowers.

4005 Old U.S. 395 North, North Washoe Valley
washoecounty.us/parks/specialty_facilities/bowers_mansion.php

HAVE A FAIRY TALE EXPERIENCE
AT CHICKADEE RIDGE

You know that scene in *Cinderella*—or is it *Snow White* (or both?)—where birds delicately land on the princess's outstretched finger? Well, this is hard to manage in real life. Except on Chickadee Ridge overlooking Lake Tahoe.

The ridge itself rises above Tahoe Meadows, just southwest of Mount Rose. It's a fairly easy, two-mile-ish climb with a beautiful payoff: views from the summit reveal the splendor of Lake Tahoe and the mountains to the west.

But the best part of the experience—particularly if you're snowshoeing in winter months to get there—involves the birds. Chickadee Ridge is thusly named because of the prevalence of the adorable tiny birds, who hang out in the lodgepole and white bark pines on the ridge. As promised, they will eat wild birdseed you bring from home directly from your hand.

Just like Cinderella. Or was it Mary Poppins?

Accessed via the Mount Rose Highway (SR 431); Tahoe Meadows parking is one mile past the Mount Rose Summit

PICK A DIRECTION,
PACK SOME POLES (OR A BOARD),
AND HIT THE SLOPES

Of course no book about northern Nevada would be complete without mention of the region's winter sport of choice: skiing/boarding.

Because when Lake Tahoe is in your backyard, snow is kinda your thing. The nice part: Reno gets far less snow than lake-level, yet we can be on the slopes of fifteen ski/board/cross-country ski areas in most cases within an hour from home.

Here's a fun fact, courtesy of our convention authority: Reno/Tahoe has the highest concentration of ski and snowboard resorts in all of North America. And that means choices. If you're looking for a destination for trick s, we've got it. If you're a noob just cutting your polar teeth, our resorts have abundant bunny hills.

Plus all that snow makes for good ice-skating, sledding, snowshoeing—and ski-lodge-cocoa-sipping next to a roaring fire.

visitrenotahoe.com/reno-tahoe/what-to-do/ski/search

CULTURE AND HISTORY

EAT YOUR ART OUT
AT THE NEVADA MUSEUM OF ART

What you'll likely first notice about the Nevada Museum of Art is the drama inherent to the building's exterior. Locals celebrate it as the most resolute work of art at the museum, as the black façade, made of creased and folded zinc, is intended to emulate the rock textures found in the nearby Black Rock Desert.

Once inside, you'll be exposed to ever-diverse exhibitions (they rotate new exhibits in multiple times a year). Bottom line: locals are constantly visiting and exploring something new, unexpected, and thought provoking.

The NMA is the only accredited art museum in the state of Nevada. Don't miss a visit to the Sky Deck, the awesome gift shop, and chez louie, located on the first floor, where renowned chef and restaurateur Mark Estee brings friendly French-inspired cuisine to museum guests.

160 W Liberty St., 775-329-3333
nevadaart.org

CHANNEL YOUR INNER BOB ROSS
AT PICASSO & WINE

If you've ever thought to yourself, "Maybe a tree lives right there" while admiring a painting, Picasso & Wine is the place for you. And better yet: a glass of wine can be consumed as you decide where your happy trees live.

At Picasso & Wine, Reno's first paint-and-sip, you'll walk in to find a canvas ready to be transformed. After ordering a cocktail (or two—heck, you'll be there for a few hours), you'll get step-by-step instructions from spunky yet capable artists.

Best of all, you'll go home with your painting in hand AND a newfound appreciation for art. And the end product? Well, you can either donate it to charity, proudly display it on your personal wall of fame/shame, or gift it at your next White Elephant exchange. Look at you, being all ahead of the gift-giving game!

Picasso & Wine
Midtown Location, 148 Vassar St., 775-453-1168
Summit Mall Location, 13925 S Virginia St. Ste. 248, 775-360-6664
picasso-wine.com

FIND FUN ON THE FARM
AT ANDELIN FAMILY FARM

If you're lucky enough to be in town during certain seasons, Andelin Family Farm is worth a special visit. This family-owned farm in Spanish Springs allows you to get up close and personal with baby animals during Baby Animal Days, usually spanning a few weekends in the springtime. What could be better than spending the day with chicks, ducklings, bunnies, piglets, lambs, goat kids, and calves?

The farm also hosts a summer kids' farm camp, field trips, and special events, and sells farm-raised meats and produce.

And of course, the Fall Festival Pumpkin Patch allows you to pick your own pumpkin and take advantage of fun activities like a hayride, cow train, lassoing, hay bale maze for kids, "cow milking," and farm games. And for older kids: the popular Corn Creepers Haunted Attraction and Zombie Paintball are reasons to come.

8100 Pyramid Way, Sparks, 775-530-8032
andelinfamilyfarm.com

WALK ON CLOUDS
AT THE DISCOVERY MUSEUM

Where can you walk on clouds, view your own veins from the inside out, and do a face swap with a bighorn sheep to e-mail to friends and family? Only one place that we know of: the Terry Lee Wells Nevada Discovery Museum, known to locals as the Discovery.

Visitors ranging in age from one to one hundred can explore the Discovery, a world-class, hands-on science center that sits at the intersection of culture and education, offering exhibits and activities to keep minds thriving.

This is likely not the "typical" museum experience of your early education; in fact, you'll climb, touch, explore, stretch, and grow your brain with fascinating facts—most about Nevada and the West.

The calendar is full of events for children, teens, educators, and parents; this Discovery is well worth it.

490 S Center St., 775-786-1000
nvdm.org

GET A DELIVERY FROM MARS
IN THE UNR KNOWLEDGE CENTER

While it's not directly from space, the MARS experience on campus at the University of Nevada, Reno does feel otherworldly. The Mathewson Automated Retrieval System—MARS—is just one of the highlights of the Knowledge Center, a library and location for all things digital on campus. This high-tech contraption houses multiple floors of the older, low-use books and journals in the library, robotically retrieving these materials upon request.

Once you've received your book or journal from MARS, explore the Knowledge Center, head up to the Joe (UNR's student union) for a bite to eat, then explore the campus of the state's oldest college, which was relocated from Elko to Reno in 1885. From the majestic quad to the brand new School of Medicine, there is much to be seen on the Nevada campus.

University of Nevada, Reno
664 N Virginia St., 775-784-1110
unr.edu

TIP

Don't miss Morrill Hall on the south end of the quad, the campus's original building constructed in 1885.

TAKE A DRIVE ON THE WILD SIDE
AT THE NATIONAL AUTOMOBILE MUSEUM

You likely don't know that actor James Dean drove a 1949 Mercury Series 9CM Six-Passenger Coupe in the 1955 movie *Rebel Without a Cause*. Nor would you know that a 1907 Thomas Flyer won the famous 1908 New York to Paris auto race.

But you would know these fun facts after seeing these historic cars firsthand at the National Automobile Museum.

If you're a car lover, a fan of celebrities, or just a casual admirer of history, this museum puts you in the driver's seat as you explore more than two hundred historic cars among authentic street scenes and sounds.

The majority of the museum's cars are from the world-famous collection of the late Bill Harrah, patriarch of the Harrah family—namesake of the casino hotel chain that got its start just around the corner in downtown Reno.

10 S Lake St., 775-333-9300
automuseum.org

WALK THROUGH TIME
WITH A HISTORIC RENO
PRESERVATION SOCIETY TOUR

While Reno earned early fame as the quickie divorce capital, these early days invited historically significant players to live and play in our neighborhoods. Celebrated actors, feared mobsters, and renowned architects were among some of Reno's earliest residents and cultural contributors.

The Historic Reno Preservation Society hosts walking tours exploring different aspects of Reno's early days. One tour explores cemeteries and their notable "residents"; another, the homes and buildings designed by famous architect Frederic DeLongchamps; still another, locations in movies like *The Misfits, Cobb, Sister Act,* and *Love Ranch*, as well as a chance to walk in the footsteps of Marilyn Monroe, Kirk Douglas, Kevin Costner, and Clint Eastwood, among others, who've roamed our streets.

So pick up the pace: walk (don't run) on a guided tour exploring Reno's rich history.

775-747-4478
historicreno.org

HUNT FOR GHOSTS
AT THE GOLD HILL HOTEL

If you're like most visitors to Reno, you'll visit Virginia City, exploring Comstock Lode history while traveling up and down its iconic wood-planked main street.

But one mile south of Virginia City on Highway 342 is a completely authentic, rooted-in-the-past experience: the Gold Hill Hotel, established in 1861 and renowned as Nevada's oldest operating hotel.

The hotel's original stone structure, erected two years after the town was settled in 1861, still houses four rooms; a 1987 addition offers larger and more contemporary amenities. So guests can pick their poison.

And speaking of: a fire just outside of one of the original rooms killed thirty-nine miners in 1869, meaning that this is a regular haunt for famous and novice paranormal investigators.

Yeah, the pun there was totally intended.

Don't miss the property's bar, a popular gathering place for Virginia City old-timers and their stories, as well as an upscale onsite restaurant.

1540 Main St., Gold Hill, 775-847-0111
goldhillhotel.net

DON YOUR COMFY SHOES
FOR ART SPOT RENO'S MIDTOWN MURAL TOUR

Street art is a burgeoning movement in northern Nevada, which led the local nonprofit arts advocacy group Art Spot Reno to develop a Midtown Mural Tour. You can download the map yourself and explore the region, or participate in a two-hour guided tour, most often happening the second Saturday of each month.

All told, the area has about seventy colorful murals painted by local, national, and international artists. On the guided tour, you'll learn about the artists and their history, the murals and their symbolism, all from informed docents eager to share their knowledge.

Oh, and be prepared: many of the murals are located in alleys, so get ready to venture out and discover Reno's truly hidden artistic gems.

artspotreno.com/midtown-mural-tour

SET THE STAGE FOR HISTORIC FUN
AT PIPER'S OPERA HOUSE

What do Mark Twain, Errol Flynn, Al Jolson, and Hal Holbrook all have in common? They've all graced the stage of Piper's Opera House in Virginia City.

While not a theatrical venue with a widespread reputation, its pedigree as a significant theater attracting national and international stars is long storied. From the 1860s until the 1920s, the theater's spotlight fell on some of the most famous faces of stage and screen.

Now it is a working museum with seasonal public tours supporting the daily operations of the house. Performances on the stage still happen on occasion, as restoration of the grand structure continues.

And worthy of note: The Old Corner Bar, located on the ground-floor level in the front corner of the building, is open year round and attracts its fair share of Virginia City characters.

12 North B St., Virginia City, 775-847-0433
facebook.com/pipersoperahouse

CALL "ALL ABOARD"
ON THE V&T RAILROAD

During the Comstock Lode, when gold and silver were abundant in the surrounding hills, trains like the V&T—or Virginia and Truckee—used to traverse back and forth from mountains to valleys, transporting the wealth. That's why it's called "Queen of the Shortlines"—its route wasn't long, but the haul was intense.

Today, you can still travel back in time to the bonanza days on the V&T Railroad. Authentic steam engines will take you on scenic rides between Carson City and Virginia City or Virginia City and Gold Hill, or you can explore the Carson River Canyon.

The rides happen seasonally, with some holiday specials— including the popular Polar Express™ during the holiday season. It doesn't get much better than an old steam engine, hot cocoa, and Santa.

For an authentic Old West experience, there's perhaps no better ride than the V&T.

877-RAIL-007 or 877-724-5007
vtrailway.com

TAKE A PAGE FROM HISTORY
IN THE DOWNTOWN RENO LIBRARY

For many locals, their childhood weekends were spent scampering among the many floors and sprawling stacks of the Downtown Reno Library, which has seemingly stood frozen in time since its opening. The building, constructed in 1966, still maintains a retro vibe that, when combined with the smell of old books and newsprint, brings some Renoites right back to those early, simpler days.

This branch of the library system still stands as an iconic literary hub, and its architecture and design are a thing to behold. According to library lore, architect Hewitt Wells wasn't allowed to place the library in a park as he'd hoped, so the library's interior was loaned a park-like feel. Hundreds of lush green plants, several full-grown trees, and a pond with a fountain all occupy the building's interior.

301 S Center St., 775-327-8300
washoecountylibrary.us/libraries/downtown-reno.php

FEEL THE BURN (AND WIND) AT BURNING MAN

Whatever you think you know about Burning Man, chances are, you're not wrong. But you're also not right. The weeklong gathering, which takes place in the Black Rock Desert about two hundred miles from Reno, is part public art festival, part social experiment, part spiritual exploration, and part counterculture statement.

Ultimately, it's a network of people inspired by shared values and united in the pursuit of a more creative and connected existence in the world. Oh, and they burn a giant wooden man at the end.

Got it? Didn't think so.

Bottom line: you have to experience it to understand it. So grab a bike, about forty-five cases of water, bandanas to cover your mouth and nose against the relentless blowing sand, some "colorful" attire, and head to Black Rock City, the only city in the world constructed and then deconstructed within a few weeks' span.

Black Rock Desert
burningman.org

LEARN FROM OLD WORLD CULINARY MASTERS
AT ARTE ITALIA

The art of fine cooking is often ignored in traditional "arts" programing, but not so in Reno. Arte Italia is a hotspot for culinary connoisseurs, an opportunity where guests can learn techniques and recipes from authentic Italian chefs.

The brick mansion housing the experience is located along the arts corridor in the Old Southwest, an appropriately historic venue. Arte Italia is seen as Nevada's premier Italian Cultural Arts Center, dedicated to preserving the traditions and heritage of old Italy through programming and exhibitions.

Throughout the year, distinguished chefs from Italy are announced, their classes including a mix of traditional and contemporary cuisine from the chef's region. Participants are chosen lottery style from among those who've submitted their names for inclusion; there is a fee for each class.

The gallery space often hosts exhibits as well; those are free and open to the public during business hours.

442 Flint St., 775-333-0313
arteitaliausa.com

EXPLORE EXOTIC ARTIFACTS AND GARDENS
AT THE WILBUR D. MAY CENTER

Anyone from Reno who has ever been on a museum field trip as a child can tell you where to find the shrunken head. Trust us, we're still traumatized.

But the Wilbur D. May Museum has much more than just a creepy shrunken head and abundant taxidermy (though that's what we likely recall most). The museum is all about the legacy of mid-20th-century Reno businessman/philanthropist Wilbur D. May. The permanent collection highlights exotic artifacts from his forty travels around the world, his business, and his life.

Outside, the adjacent arboretum comprises twenty-three acres, thirteen of it serving as a living plant museum with more than four thousand native and adaptive plant species on display.

This is a truly unforgettable museum experience highlighting an important pillar of the community. But seriously, the eyelashes on that shrunken head . . .

1595 N Sierra St. (inside Rancho San Rafael Regional Park), 775-785-5961
washoecounty.us/parks/maycenterhome/museum/index.php

WALK
IN THE FOOTSTEPS OF THE DOOMED DONNER PARTY

It's rare that a destination allows you to camp, fish, hike, boat, and stargaze, as well as learn about one of the most significantly disastrous human pioneer stories in the history of the West.

But that's exactly what happens at Donner Lake.

Visitors go for Donner Lake's outdoor recreational offerings, which are incredible—but many are captivated by the true cultural and learning experience at the memorial and visitors center. There you'll find the Pioneer Monument, which was built in the early 1900s in honor of all who made the trek across the plains and mountains to reach California during the Gold Rush of the 1840s. And the museum's exhibits provide insights into the plight of the Donner family and similar emigrants.

Donner Memorial State Park and Emigrant Trail Museum
12593 Donner Pass Rd. at Highway 80, Truckee, CA, 530-582-7892
parks.ca.gov/?page_id=503

TIP

While admiring the bronze Pioneer Monument, consider this: the stone pedestal is twenty-two feet high, the same depth as the snow that imprisoned the ill-fated Donner Party for four months. Out of the eighty-seven emigrants who embarked on the wagon train, only forty-eight were rescued the following spring. Survivors provided accounts of starvation and of some of the group resorting to cannibalism.

EXPLORE
RENO'S OVERARCHING SLOGAN WITH A TRIP DOWNTOWN

Think "Reno," and you'll likely conjure images of the iconic arch and the town's slogan: "Biggest Little City in the World." And the fact is, the arch and the slogan are co-stars in a historic tale of community pride.

The first arch was built in 1926, with the slogan added after a public contest in 1929. Over the decades, Reno has grappled with the question: is the slogan relevant or outdated? But locals now almost universally embrace it and its meaning, quickly pointing out that Reno truly has a classic, small-town vibe with big-city amenities. It serves as a physical reminder that Reno offers the best of both worlds.

And speaking of both worlds: Both an original arch and a modern one grace our downtown: the historic version over Center Street near the National Automobile Museum and the modern version over Virginia Street in the heart of downtown.

BROWSE ARTIFACTS IN MINT CONDITION
AT THE NEVADA STATE MUSEUM

What good is a region built on silver without its own mint, right? City leadership came to that very conclusion back in 1870, establishing the Carson City Mint in our state capital.

While the mint only ran for nineteen years, many of its artifacts remain in the Nevada State Museum. But the destination is more than solely a historical look at silver; it also houses native American art and a full-sized skeleton of a Columbian mammoth, as well as a locals' favorite: a replica of a ghost town and an underground mine.

The Nevada State Museum has been open and celebrating the state's natural and cultural history since 1941. It also showcases the importance of Native Americans and Basque, Chinese, and Latino immigrants and their impact on community and culture.

600 N Carson St., Carson City, 775-687-4810
museums.nevadaculture.org/nsmcc

VISIT
NEVADA'S CROWNING GLORY: OUR STATE CAPITOL IN CARSON CITY

In the dead center of Carson City stands a statuesque building with a glistening silver dome. And all who travel through the town regard it as the ultimate Nevada symbol: our State Capitol, a must-visit destination.

In 1870, six years after Nevada entered the union, the structure was constructed in a large lot in the center of town—the region's forefathers accurately predicting the future growth that would occur. To moderate costs, the building's sandstone was obtained free of charge from the Nevada State Prison quarry, just outside Carson City.

History resonates throughout the building, and the public is invited to conduct self-guided tours during operating hours. It is the second oldest capitol building west of the Mississippi River, and every Nevada governor except the first has had his office in the capitol.

101 N Carson St., Carson City
visitcarsoncity.com/thingstodocarsoncity/capitol-building

TIP
Explore the entire capitol campus,
which includes the State Capitol, Legislative
Building, Supreme Court, and State Library
and Archives.

SCOUR
A LOCAL MAGAZINE

If you truly want to get a sense of the current cultural conversations happening in northern Nevada, perhaps no resource is more relevant than the abundant community-centric publications that employ storytelling as a means of education and inspiration.

We have specialty magazines that are serving a variety of niches—from the upscale reflections found in *RENO Magazine* to the food-focused publication known as *Edible Reno-Tahoe*; from the warm community hugs called *Bliss Babe* and *I Love Reno* to *Reno Tahoe Tonight's* spotlight on entertainment; from the family focus in the pages of *Reno Moms Blog* to the tongue-in-cheek *Reno Memo*.

And these are just a sampling of publications highlighting Reno. Browse Nevada newsstands or websites, and you're bound to see pages devoted to local culture.

So make like a journalist, and start researching: pick up/scan a local magazine, read about the town's latest offerings, and be inspired to explore!

VISIT
RENO'S MOST MOBILE HOME: THE LAKE MANSION

Longtime Reno residents have likely seen the Lake Mansion traveling down Virginia Street—not only once, but maybe even twice. That's because the building, known as Reno's "first address," has been located on three different properties.

It was first built by the founder of Reno, Myron Lake, who operated a toll bridge across Virginia Street. But as the building went into disrepair, supporters raised funds to move it to land outside the current Convention Center. And then, in 2004, it was moved back closer to its original home, now on the corner of Court and Arlington.

Visit the Lake Mansion to get a sense of Reno's first address—two addresses later. But also explore the cultural opportunities happening with Arts for All Nevada, its current occupant. The nonprofit offers quality arts programming for all abilities and ages.

Arts for All Nevada
250 Court St., 775-826-6100
artsforallnevada.org

SHOPPING AND FASHION

CENTER IN
ON RENO'S MIDTOWN

When we're talking unique retail destinations in Reno, nine out of ten locals agree: Midtown is the place to be! (And that tenth person doesn't like cool stuff, so she doesn't matter.)

Midtown is growing in all directions, with new construction happening around Sticks on Virginia and new boutiques practically popping up daily in the core. The only constant among the unique, local, diverse businesses: a focus on friendly people serving distinct niches through mostly boutique solutions.

So our advice: walk Midtown. Start on Virginia somewhere to the south of the downtown core, then just explore the various open doors you'll find along the way.

Here are a few to get you started.

Junkee Clothing Exchange

This is fifteen thousand square feet of fun and funky clothes, recycled awesomeness, and affordable antiques and furniture.

960 S Virginia St., 775-322-5865
junkeeclothingexchange.com

Happy Happy Joy Joy

Just walking into this store will make you unspeakably happy—the colors, the toys, the retro vibe, the pop culture feel, the gag gifts, the endless clever stuff, the TOYS!!!

23 Martin St., 775-562-1113
happyhappyreno.com

Natural Selection

Succulents, fossils, quirky taxidermy, and other natural curiosities, presented with a sense of humor and an underlying appreciation for the environment.

39 Saint Lawrence Ave., 775-376-2282
facebook.com/naturalselectionstore

Sierra Belle

Fierce, urban, chic, affordable, and practical fashion finds, all wrapped up in a downhome, support-your-fellow-female kinda vibe.

The Sticks Shopping Center, 726 S Virginia St., 775-470-8390
shopsierrabelle.com

FEEL RIGHT AT HOME
IN THESE UNIQUE FURNITURE STORES

Looking for something way outside of the big-box furniture experience? Take some time to explore these local treasures.

Not Just Furniture is a family-owned business with an inviting, no-pressure showroom full of secondhand furniture and home décor—mostly from estates. This is not consignment, but rather straight sale at crazy-affordable prices. Need something unusual to serve as the ultimate conversation piece for your home? You might just find a slot machine, yard art in the form of a purple metal armadillo, or a mid-century Danish teak armoire here. Check back often for new selections.

The Find, also locally owned and operated, is a roomy warehouse of brand new, handpicked, and stylish home décor. Inviting, beautiful furniture is offered here at warehouse prices. Beyond the exquisite furniture selection is a store-within-a-store, ThreadSS, featuring candles, gifts, jewelry, and accessories.

Not Just Furniture
500 East Moana Ln. Ste. A, 775-825-4515
notjustfurniturereno.com

The Find
4865 Longley Ln. #D, 775-322-3463
thefindreno.com

CHOOSE YOUR OWN ADVENTURE
IN AREA BOOKSTORES

You've heard rumor that neighborhood bookstores are remnants of a bygone era? Not true in Reno. We have a thriving independent bookstore scene spearheaded by two totally different literary experiences.

The first thing you'll notice about Sundance Bookstore: THAT BUILDING! The Levy House (errr, mansion) was constructed in 1906 and is listed in the U.S. Register of Historic Places. The building features a grand staircase, gleaming parquet floors, and rich details. Then: THE SELECTION! Sundance offers new and used books, magazines, gifts, greeting cards, local artists' works, journals, CDs, and more. They specialize in Nevada authors, unusual books, and hard-to-find books and music.

Grassroots Books is a local gem featuring forty-thousand-plus books with a constantly changing inventory of used and new selections. New books are fifty to ninety percent off list price, bestsellers twenty percent off list price, used books starting at nintey-nine cents, huge sales every month, toys—even free book days!

Grassroots Books, 660 E Grove St., 775-828-2665
grassrootsbooks.com

Sundance Bookstore, 121 California Ave., 775-786-1188
sundancebookstore.com

ENJOY A PEAK RETAIL EXPERIENCE
AT THE SUMMIT

Visitors to this upscale, outdoor lifestyle mall routinely comment on the year-round, overflowing flowerpots that always seem meticulously maintained. This detail may seem insignificant, but it's the details that set the Summit apart from a typical mall experience.

This is the largest concentration in town of tried, true, and trusted retail names: Dillard's, Apple, lululemon athletica, Pottery Barn, MAC, Old Navy, and more. Plus it's anchored by Century Theatres, meaning you can get your shop on before indulging in popcorn, soft drinks, and the latest Hollywood blockbuster.

The mall's modern design offers beautiful pathways connecting stores with nature—sculptures and manicured landscape make browsers feel right at home. Holiday events, fashion shows, and summer farmers markets further connect the community to the Summit experience.

13925 South Virginia St., 775-853-7800
thesummitonline.com

HAVE A
SPA-TACULAR TIME
AT TOP-NOTCH RESORTS

You're in the mood for some pampering—a full day devoted to you. Sounds sublime, right? Well luckily, these two resorts offer the perfect prescription for daylong rejuvenation.

Peppermill Resort Spa Casino's Spa Toscana comprises three stories (yup, three) and thirty-three thousand square feet of spa space bathed in Mediterranean beauty.

There, you'll relax in the nation's only caldarium that includes an indoor pool, sun deck, and secret garden. Twenty-four treatment rooms offer healthful and revolutionary spa treatments.

Spa Atlantis is Reno's only Forbes Four-Star Luxury Spa, with thirty thousand square feet of space and amenities like three co-ed lounges, fifteen luxurious treatment rooms, year-round indoor whirlpools, and an atrium pool, along with an outdoor pool and whirlpool.

Known for its exquisite treatments and couples spa experiences, this spa also has unique options like eastern Asian massage, a Mineral Mud Ceremony, and a Cleopatra Milk and Honey Cocoon.

Peppermill Resort Spa Casino's Spa Toscana
2707 S Virginia St., 775-689-7190, spatoscana.com

Spa Atlantis, 3800 S Virginia St., 775-954-4135
atlantiscasino.com/spa

STEP BACK IN TIME
IN VIRGINIA CITY

As you shuffle along the authentic wood-planked paths of Virginia City, admiring the detailed and historic façades of the surrounding buildings, you'll be surprised by the variety of retail options you encounter. Shops with native jewelry and stones, mercantiles with Old West souvenirs, and Western-style clothing and accessories are the norm, obviously. But so are beautiful antiques, as well as places to pose for old-time photos—the latter being a favorite among children who want to play dress up.

Don't miss Grandma's Fudge Factory, a Virginia City institution. And be on the lookout for the bearded gentleman, dressed in a period hat and suspenders, alongside his burro—both of whom look as though they just stepped right out of a Comstock Lode mine.

Virginia City Tourism Commission
86 South C St., Virginia City, 1-800-718-SLVR (7587), 775-847-7500
visitvirginiacitynv.com/attractions/shopping

KEEP IT ALL IN THE FAMILY
AT LOCAL SHOPS

If you're looking for a distinctly family-friendly, welcoming vibe when you walk into a local shop, read on. These locales exude a charm and warmth that is reminiscent of a bygone era. Yet they also have super-cool inventory!

Purple Avocado: Walk through the purple door to meet owners Sue and Stan Jones, who have recreated that iconic gift shop experience that used to grace Anytown, USA. Explore this colorful and historic home, built in 1863, to find your next treasure.

Freckled Frog: Michael and Sue Murphy have created a uniquely rich retail store experience, offering stylish, eclectic, and affordable home accessories as well as antiques.

The Nest: Owner Tessa Dee Miller has created a refuge for beautiful vintage heirlooms, clothing, furniture, and accessories. Even the window displays will make you swoon.

Purple Avocado, 904 N Curry St., Carson City, 775-883-6233
thepurpleavocado.com

Freckled Frog, 45 Foothill Rd. Ste. 3, 775-453-1777
thefreckledfrogreno.com

The Nest, 201 Keystone Ave., 775-284-8841
thenestreno.com

FEEL RIGHT AT HOME
IN ARLINGTON GARDENS

For those who visited Arlington Gardens Mall in its heyday, you'll remember warm vibes and smells wafting throughout the space, a charming peacefulness reflected through every locally owned boutique. That seemed to have disappeared—until now. It's easy to see that Arlington Gardens is springing back to life while paying homage to its colorful past. The bones of the building stay intact, the bricks are still under foot, but new and exciting changes are clearly on the horizon!

In fact, at the time of this book's publication, signs promising the Rattlesnake Club, a new restaurant to make its home right inside the front doors, are on display. Boutique owners tell of a full bar, a wine cellar, outdoor patios and fire pits, fresh-roasted coffee, unique entrees, and abundant parking. We can't wait!

Until then, at right are just a few of the retail gems helping to usher in Arlington Gardens' new era.

Arlington Gardens
606 W Plumb Ln.

Larkellen

This boutique beams with local pride—from its signature Nevada trucker hats to state-shaped signage that can readily grace any Nevada abode to clothes for men and women. The mother-daughter owners scour their surroundings for eco-conscious, locally sourced merchandise. Be prepared to buy something for anyone who loves Nevada—which likely includes you! Merchandise changes frequently, so check back often.

775-825-5002
larkellenreno.com

Cooking Gallery

This place is an oasis of quirky, practical, and hard-to-find gifts for the gourmet foodie in your life. High-end cooking tools and utensils, signature pottery for tables and cabinets, knives galore, an endless wall of gadgets—it's all here and ripe for the picking.

775-470-8008

BROWSE THE FRUITS (AND VEGETABLES)
OF LOCAL LABOR AT FARMERS MARKETS

From spring to fall in northern Nevada, the sun usually shines down on a variety of farmers markets, which sometimes pop up in totally unexpected places. Church parking lots, strip malls, casino/resorts, and major retail destinations all play host to area growers looking to sell their goods.

And the selection isn't limited to fresh produce—though that's certainly the centerpiece and most coveted aspect of each stand. You'll also find arts and crafts, locally made gifts, and novelties. Farmers may offer samples or cooking demonstrations, and live music is often a draw.

All in all, a farmers market is an ideal destination for fun, regardless of your age.

visitrenotahoe.com/reno-tahoe/what-to-do/shopping/farmers-markets

TIP

While browsing different vendors, look for signs touting "Nevada Grown"; these are area farmers who call the Silver State home.

MEET LOCAL LEGENDS
AT THE OUTLETS AT SPARKS

While we don't often associate retail therapy with the idea of expanding our brains, that's exactly the delicate balance struck at the Outlets at Sparks. The outdoor mall is perfect for history buffs who also enjoy shopping, considering metal tributes to Nevada legends dot the landscape. Intricate, sometimes whimsical sculptures honor such figures as Mark Twain and Pony Express riders.

The Outlets at Sparks is also a great place for kids and their parents, especially in warm months, when fountains entertain children (bring a suit and a towel) and parents can sit on benches overlooking the fun.

And we haven't even mentioned the shopping yet! Comprising mostly outlets, the mall has Old Navy Outlet, Loft Outlet, Banana Republic Factory Store, and Nike Factory Store, among others.

Oh yeah, and there's Scheels! And an IMAX theater! The Outlets really is a remarkable collection of awesome.

1310 Scheels Dr., Sparks, 775-358-3800
outletsatsparks.com

GO PLUMB CRAZY
ON RENO'S PLUMB LANE

Plumb Lane connects historic parts of Reno with its downtown, a fact that lends some understanding to the retail experiences there: eclectic, charming, all unique.

In a shopping center called Plumbgate, you'll find Chez Vous, which offers upscale but down-to-earth women's clothing, home décor, and gifts.

Another stop in Plumbgate (though there are SO MANY MORE!) is Couture Closet, where industry stylists will personally help you find pieces to reflect your signature style.

Further east down Plumb toward the airport is the Niche, a locals' favorite boutique with affordable, one-of-a-kind home accessories and creative gifts.

Chez Vous, 538 W Plumb Ln. Ste. C, 775-826-4948

Couture Closet, 538 W Plumb Ln. Ste. E, 775-432-1869
thecouticureclosetreno.com

The Niche, 1300 E Plumb Ln., 775-348-8661
shoptheniche.com

BREATHE IN THE FLOWER POWER
AT CHARMING FLORAL BOUTIQUES

In search of a gift direct from Mother Nature? How about some lavender for cooking or a beautifully potted indoor arrangement? Here are a few totally organic options:

Lavender Ridge is a family-owned and -operated lavender farm just outside of Reno. You can order its products online any time, and it also has limited retail times on-site. Choose from hand-crafted lavender products including bath and body items, candles, soaps, culinary seasonings, herbal teas, and more.

Browse Moana Nursery's Moana Lane Garden Center to find a wide selection of flowers, unique gifts, and stuff for the garden. If you're looking for a gift for the green thumb in your life (or maybe it's you?), this fragrant shop has stunning indoor plants in its greenhouse; pottery, garden, and patio accessories; gifts; fountains; and statuary.

Lavender Ridge, 7450 W 4th St., 775-747-3222
lavenderridgereno.com

Moana Nursery, 1100 W Moana Ln., 775-825-0602
moananursery.com

GO LOCO LOCO
FOR SHOPS THAT ARE LOCAL LOCAL

We Nevadans LOVE our state. And as such, we also love shops that sell Nevada-themed merchandise. We've already suggested Larkellen (page 113), but here are a few other places to fill those Nevada-themed gift bags.

Nevada Legislative Gift Shop: With many visitors walking through the door to experience our biennial legislature, this gift shop in Carson City answers the need for souvenirs for visitors. Most items incorporate Nevada symbols—the "Battle Born" insignia, for example, or products representing emblems recognized as "official" by statute: the desert bighorn sheep (official state animal), the desert tortoise (official state reptile), and mountain bluebird (official state bird).

Reno Envy is a store, a brand, and a lifestyle with a distinct personality. Most merchandise sports the iconic trailer logo, which celebrates Reno's outdoor lifestyle while poking fun at our community's humble roots. This is a great destination for hoodies, tees, hats, and so much more.

Nevada Legislative Gift Shop, 401 S Carson St., Carson City, 775-684-6835
leg.state.nv.us/app/lcbstore/a/default.aspx

Reno Envy, 135 N Sierra St., 775-682-3800
renoenvy.com

SAY "CALIFORNIA, HERE I COME"
TO VISIT TRUCKEE'S UNIQUE SHOPPING SCENE

Truckee was built on a railroad, and that rustic charm is reflective along the main downtown corridor. Charming Downtown Truckee has fun and funky shops that pay homage to the town's gritty history and vibrant present.

Here are just a few to watch for as you browse:

Bespoke, which descriptively sells "stuff and things" (that's how they characterize themselves, which we love). You'll find vintage, kitschy, and a whole lot of amazing here.

High Camp Home sells rustic furniture, gorgeous accessories, and cabin-style influences. This is where you'll find bear themes and all things "outdoor" that you want to bring in.

Truckee Variety Co. is brimming with games, toys, and fun accessories that will please kids—or adults who still love to play.

Bespoke, 10130 Donner Pass Rd., Truckee, CA, 530-582-5500
bespoketruckee.com

High Camp Home, 10191 Donner Pass Rd., Truckee, CA, 530-582-6866
highcamphome.com

Truckee Variety Co., 10088 Donner Pass Rd., Truckee, CA, 530-587-3117

● ●

SATISFY YOUR INNER FOODIE
AT NOTHING TO IT

Nothing To It Culinary Center is like Disneyland for people who love food. The quaint kitchen store has a huge selection of tools, utensils, and gadgets. Warning: browsing the selection may actually convince you that you need things you didn't even know existed (the author may or may not have a "flexicado" avocado slicer, just as one example).

The store is really a gateway to the Nothing To It cooking school, which offers regular classes on a variety of amazing topics. There's a night for artisan pizza, sushi, dim sum, gumbo, and more. And if it's technique you're looking to master: some classes cover knife skills, modern pressure cookers, cast iron—even cooking with wine (we're fairly sure you don't need help with that, but it never hurts to brush up).

Go for a visit to browse the store, then visit the calendar online and book a class, which is a perfect night out with friends.

Especially classes with wine. Just sayin'.

225 Crummer Ln., 775-826-2628
nothingtoit.com

MAKE A JOURNEY
DOWN TO THE BASEMENT

This is certainly not the creepy, mildew-scented basement of your childhood home. Instead, it's an unexpected shopping experience situated beneath the historic 1933 U.S. Post Office in downtown Reno. This underground venue is a hip and modern marketplace, one that is constantly evolving to meet its mission: a multi-use incubator space of both retail and food vendors who celebrate the craft of the hand.

Get thee to the basement. Seriously. You won't be disappointed.

50 S Virginia St., 775-848-2248
thebasementreno.com

A FEW HIGHLIGHTS

- West Elm actually sits on top of the Basement, but this modern home décor store has stylish and contemporary pieces.
- Rawbry is a cold-pressed juice bar, serving nutrient-packed beverages that are alarmingly tasty.
- Global Coffee is a friendly, locally owned coffee bar that also happens to have unforgettable hot chocolate.
- Sugar Love Chocolates uses real ingredients from around the world to create unique flavor combinations.
- Chomp is a made-to-order Reno salad bar supporting local agriculture and sustainable practices.

SUGGESTED
ITINERARIES

Chances are, you have different interests and goals for planning your outings. Below, find suggestions for activities based on what you may be trying to accomplish. Warning: Please spread these activities out; trying these all in one sitting could be hazardous to your health.

ROMANTIC AND/OR FASCINATING FIRST-DATE DINING

Casale's Halfway Club, 2

Campo, 31

Twisted Fork, 7

Calafuria, 11

Zozo's Ristorante, 18

The Depot, 17

La Vecchia, 22

The Coney, 9

Rapscallion, 30

The Ritz-Carlton Lake Tahoe and Northstar, 59

FOR YOUR FAVORITE FOODIE

A DAY OF PAMPERING

Social Hour at Bistro Napa, 23

Swill Coffee & Wine, 33

Rawbry, 123

Too Soul Tea Co., 33

Spa Atlantis or Spa Toscana, 109

Shop Midtown, 104

Brose a local bookstore at Sundance or Grassroots, 107

Great Full Gardens, 27

Global Coffee, 123

Sunday Music Brunch or First Thursday at Nevada Museum
of Art, 52

FEELING FRISKY

Reno Riverwalk District Wine Walk, 5

Attend a beer/pub crawl, 32

Picon Punch at Louis' Basque Corner, Santa Fe, or
J T Basque Bar, 6

LEX Nightclub, 38

Sangria or margaritas at Los Compadres, 8

Death & Taxes, 16

• •

NOT-YOUR-TYPICAL GIFT IDEAS

FURNITURE AND HOME DÉCOR

• •

NEVADA TREASURES

EVENTS
BY SEASON

Some of the activities listed in this book are seasonal; see below for ideas about when to check some of these items off your Reno bucket list.

SPRING

Andelin Family Farm Baby Animal Days, 80

Bowers Mansion, 73

Hunter Creek Trail, 60

Reno Aces, 57

Reno Food Tours, 15

SUMMER

Artown, 39

Bartley Ranch, 42

Bowers Mansion, 73

Burning Man, 91

Farmers markets, 114

Feed the Camel, 21

INDEX